southern cooking

Beverly LeBlanc
and Philip Back

p

This is a Parragon Publishing Book
First published in 2005

Parragon Publishing
Queen Street House
4 Queen Street
Bath BA1 1HE
United Kingdom

Produced by The Bridgewater Book Company

Photographer Emma Neish
Home Economist Joy Skipper

ISBN 1-40544-644-7

Printed in China

NOTE This book uses imperial, metric, or US cup measurements. Follow the same units of
measurement throughout; do not mix imperial and metric. All spoon measurements are level:
teaspoons are assumed to be 5 ml, and tablespoons are assumed to be 15 ml. Unless otherwise
stated, milk is assumed to be whole, eggs and individual vegetables such as carrots are medium,
and pepper is freshly ground black pepper. Flour has been measured by dipping the cup into
the flour and leveling the top.

The times given for each recipe are an approximate guide only. The preparation times may
differ according to the techniques used by different people and the cooking times may vary
as a result of the type of oven used. Ovens should be preheated to the specified temperature.
If using a fan-assisted oven, check the manufacturer's instructions for adjusting the time
and temperature.

Recipes using raw eggs should be avoided by infants, the elderly, pregnant women,
convalescents, and anyone suffering from an illness.

contents

Southern hospitality has long been legendary throughout America, but Southern cooking was much more of a well-kept secret. It was only when cooks from south of the Mason-Dixon line traveled north and west in the 1970s and 1980s that many Americans encountered Southern cooking for the first time.

And what an exciting mix of styles and flavors go into the large melting pot that is collectively called "Southern cooking." Cajun, Creole, and soul-food recipes reflect the history of the Southern states—Alabama, Florida, Georgia, Kentucky, Louisiana, Mississippi, North and South Carolina, Tennessee, Virginia, and West Virginia.

Southern cooks traditionally borrowed and absorbed from the French, Spanish, Afro-Caribbeans, and Native Americans. And with Cajun cooks from the Louisiana bayous adding to the pot, Southern food is unlike anything eaten in any other part of America. Many of the ingredients thought of as typically Southern—chilies, greens,

introduction

okra, rice, tomatoes, and sweet potatoes and yams—are not indigenous but were introduced with the slave trade.

Both great wealth and extreme poverty have influenced the flavors of today's American South. Creole cooking has its roots in the refined French cooking of New Orleans in the 18th century. The obvious example is gumbos—hearty stews made with game, meat, poultry, seafood, or only vegetables that always start with a slow-cooked roux. And while Creole cooking is city cooking, Cajun cooking is highly spiced country cooking.

African-American cooks have played a pivotal role in the development of Southern cooking from the colonial era onward. Originating from the vegetable-rich diets of Africa and incorporating more indigenous North American ingredients, this culinary tradition began to be known as "soul food" during the expansion of the Civil Rights movement in the 1960s.

To sample Southern hospitality at its finest, mix up a batch of Mint Juleps and let convivial conversation flow.

Mealtimes are the focal part of the day for many Southerners, but nowhere more so than in New Orleans, with its tradition of fine restaurants. Stylish Oysters Rockefeller and Shrimp Rémoulade are two favorites, and the city's two-fisted sandwiches, Po' Boys and Muffulettas, are meals in themselves. To add a Southern dimension to any occasion, try a Creamy Tuskegee Soup or a Warm Crab Dip.

appetizers, snacks & light meals

This is *the* drink of the South—and nothing epitomizes Southern hospitality like mint juleps. Traditionally, these are served in silver or pewter cups, called Jefferson cups, but tall glasses will work just as well.

mint juleps

ingredients

4–6 tsp confectioners' sugar, to taste
large handful fresh mint leaves,
 torn (not cut) into strips

about 1 tbsp premium-quality bourbon,
 plus extra to top off
crushed ice, to fill 4 tall glasses
4 fresh mint sprigs, to decorate

one Put the sugar into a nonmetallic bowl with the mint leaves. Stir in the 1 tablespoon of bourbon. Using a pestle, mash and stir the ingredients together to make a thick paste—the more you mash and the more mint leaves you use, the mintier the flavor.

two At this point, you can transfer the paste to a freezerproof container and put into the freezer for a few hours or overnight to develop a more pronounced flavor, or continue with the recipe.

three When you are ready to serve, scoop 1–1½ teaspoons of the paste into the base of each of 4 tall glasses, then fill to the top with crushed ice. Pour over enough bourbon to come to the top of the glass.

four Decorate each glass with a mint sprig and serve with a long silver spoon in the glass. Some Southern hosts noted for their generous hospitality provide a pillow per person for reclining on when guests can no longer stand.

did you know?

Mint juleps are most closely associated with the Kentucky Derby, the annual thoroughbred meeting on the first Saturday in May, at Churchill Downs, in Lexington, Kentucky. Different versions are sipped throughout the South, with brandy, rye, or rum replacing the bourbon.

Because of the laborious work involved in extracting the meat from crabs, fresh crabmeat is relatively expensive. A dip is one way to stretch the flavor, but conversely, guests will rate the party-giver on the amount of crab in the dip—the more the better.

warm **crab dip**

ingredients

1¾ cups cream cheese

3 oz/85 g medium Cheddar cheese, grated

1 cup sour cream

4 tbsp mayonnaise

2 tbsp freshly squeezed lemon juice, or to taste

2 tsp Worcestershire sauce, plus extra to taste

2 tsp Dijon mustard

1 lb 2 oz/500 g cooked fresh crabmeat, picked over, or thawed and patted dry if frozen

1 garlic clove, cut in half

butter, for greasing

salt and pepper

fresh dill sprigs, to garnish

savory crackers, to serve

one This dip tastes best if all the ingredients are mixed together 24 hours in advance to let the flavors develop, but it still tastes good if made just before serving. Put the cream cheese into a bowl and stir in the Cheddar cheese, sour cream, mayonnaise, lemon juice, Worcestershire sauce, and mustard.

two Add the crabmeat and salt and pepper to taste and gently stir together. Taste and add extra Worcestershire sauce, if desired. Cover and let chill for up to 24 hours.

three When you are ready to heat the dip, remove it from the refrigerator and let it come to room temperature. Meanwhile, preheat the oven to 350°F/180°C. Rub the cut sides of the garlic clove over the base and sides of an ovenproof dish suitable for serving from (see Step 4), then lightly grease. Spoon the crab mixture into the dish and smooth the surface. Heat the dip through in the oven for 15 minutes.

four This dip is best kept warm when served, traditionally by using a chafing dish heated by a candle. Either spoon the dip into such a dish, sprinkle with dill, and set over the heat source, or set the dip in its ovenproof dish over a fondue burner and garnish with dill. Serve with savory crackers.

did you know?

Family recipes for crab dip pass from mother to daughter in the South, along with the heirloom chafing dish, which is ideal for keeping this rich dip warm while guests mingle. Sesame seed crackers, called benne wafers, are the traditional Southern accompaniment, but any small savory cracker is fine.

The original recipe for this baked oyster dish is a guarded secret of Antoine's, New Orleans' oldest Creole restaurant, but many versions have been created. Spinach features in most of the variations.

oysters rockefeller

ingredients

24 large live oysters
rock salt
3 tbsp butter
6 scallions, chopped
1 large garlic clove, crushed
3 tbsp finely chopped celery
1½ oz/40 g watercress sprigs

1¾ cups young spinach leaves, rinsed
  and any tough stems removed
1 tbsp aniseed-flavored liqueur
4 tbsp fresh bread crumbs
few drops of hot pepper sauce, to taste
salt and pepper
lemon wedges, to serve

one Preheat the oven to 400°F/200°C. Shuck the oysters, running an oyster knife under each oyster to loosen it from its shell. Pour off the liquor. Arrange a ½–¾-inch/1–2-cm layer of salt in a roasting pan large enough to hold the oysters in a single layer, or use 2 roasting pans. Nestle the oyster shells in the salt so that they remain upright. Cover with a thick, damp dish towel and let chill while making the topping.

two If you don't have oyster plates with indentations that hold the shells upright, line 4 plates with a layer of salt deep enough to hold the shells upright. Set the plates aside.

three Melt half the butter in a large skillet over medium heat. Add the scallions, garlic, and celery and cook, stirring frequently, for 2–3 minutes, or until the vegetables are softened.

four Stir in the remaining butter, then add the watercress and spinach and cook, stirring constantly, for 1 minute, or until the leaves wilt. Transfer to a blender or small food processor and add the liqueur, bread crumbs, and hot pepper sauce and salt and pepper to taste. Whiz until well blended.

five Spoon 2–3 teaspoons of the sauce over each oyster. Bake in the oven for 20 minutes. Transfer to the prepared plates and serve with lemon wedges.

cook's tip

The exact amount of sauce needed depends on the size of the oysters—this is enough to top 24 large oysters. Any leftovers can be stirred into vegetable soups, or mixed with mayonnaise to make a sauce for sandwiches.

prepare about 15 minutes, plus 45 minutes' chilling
cook 5–8 minutes *serves* 4–6

This New Orleans classic of poached shrimp with piquant rusty-red sauce was first served at Arnaud's, one of the city's oldest restaurants. This version is from Arnaud's.

shrimp rémoulade

ingredients

1½ tbsp salt
1 lemon, sliced
1 lb 12 oz/800 g large raw
  unshelled shrimp

rémoulade sauce
2 oz/55 g scallions, coarsely chopped
2 oz/55 g celery stalks, coarsely chopped
1 large garlic clove
4 tbsp chopped fresh parsley
2 tbsp Creole mustard or
  German mustard
2 tbsp superfine sugar
2 tbsp cider vinegar or 2 tbsp
  tomato ketchup

1½ tbsp prepared horseradish
1 tbsp paprika
½ tsp cayenne pepper
½ tsp salt
¼ tsp ground black pepper
few drops of hot pepper sauce, to taste
about ⅔ cup corn or peanut oil

to serve
shredded iceberg lettuce
2 hard-cooked eggs, shelled and sliced
2 tomatoes, sliced

one To make the sauce, put the scallions, celery, garlic, and parsley into a food processor and pulse until finely chopped. Add the mustard, sugar or vinegar, ketchup, horseradish, paprika, cayenne pepper, salt, pepper, and hot pepper sauce to taste and whiz until well blended. With the motor running, slowly pour in the oil through the feed tube in a slow, steady stream until a thick, creamy sauce forms. Transfer to a large bowl, cover, and set aside.

two To poach the shrimp, bring a large pan of water with the salt and lemon slices to a boil over high heat. Add the shrimp and cook just until the shrimp turn pink.

three Drain the shrimp well and put them under cold running water until completely chilled. Shell and devein them, adding them to the sauce as you go. Stir together, then cover and let chill for at least 45 minutes, but ideally overnight. Serve on a bed of lettuce with hard-cooked eggs and sliced tomatoes.

did you know?
One of the characteristics of Creole recipes is to include French words in the titles, such as "rémoulade," even if there is little similarity with the traditional French version. Anyone expecting this sauce to taste like its creamy mustard-flavored cousin will be surprised—this rémoulade sauce is much spicier.

prepare about 15 minutes, plus 1 hour's chilling
cook no cooking   *serves* 4

While Northerners shiver through the cold winter months and comfort themselves with warming stews and casseroles, Floridians feast on fresh fruit salads. The use of fresh lime and chili gives this example a Latino flavor from Miami.

florida fruit cocktail

ingredients

1 large mango
2 large oranges
1 pink grapefruit
1 tsp finely grated lime rind
4 tbsp fresh lime juice, or to taste

1 fresh red chili, seeded and finely sliced
4 tbsp grated fresh coconut, or moist
  shredded coconut
chopped fresh cilantro, to garnish

one To prepare the mango, remove the skin from one half, then slice lengthwise down that side of the flat central seed to remove the flesh. Repeat with the other half of the fruit. Cut the flesh into bite-size portions and put into a nonmetallic bowl.

two Peel the oranges and grapefruit over the bowl, carefully removing all the bitter white pith. As each fruit is peeled, separate it into segments, cutting between the membranes and letting the segments drop into the bowl. Squeeze the juice from the membranes into the bowl.

three Stir the lime rind, lime juice, chili, and coconut into the bowl. Cover and let chill for at least 1 hour to let the flavors blend.

four Stir the fruit salad and add extra lime juice, if necessary. Spoon into bowls and sprinkle with fresh cilantro to serve.

variations

This is a mix-and-match salad that is equally good with whatever fresh tropical fruit is available—try pineapple, carambola, papaya, and even avocado. It's a refreshing first course as it is, but for a more substantial dish, add poached shrimp or crabmeat, or serve with cottage cheese.

George Washington Carver is remembered for founding The Tuskegee Institute in Alabama, in 1881, to educate African-Americans, but he is less well known for his role in the cultivation of peanuts as a cash crop in the 1890s. Peanut soup was one of the recipes he developed to promote the nutritional value of peanuts.

creamy tuskegee soup

ingredients

4 tbsp butter
1 small onion, minced
1 celery stalk, strings removed, minced
1½ tbsp all-purpose flour
3 cups chicken stock
scant ⅔ cup smooth peanut butter
pinch of cayenne pepper

¾ cup light cream
salt and pepper

to garnish
4 tbsp chopped salted peanuts
1 fresh red chili, seeded and very finely sliced
2 tbsp thinly sliced celery leaves

one Melt the butter in a pan over medium heat. Add the onion and celery and cook, stirring frequently, for 5–8 minutes until they are soft but not brown.

two Sprinkle in the flour and cook, stirring constantly, for an additional 2 minutes. Slowly stir in the stock and bring to a boil, stirring constantly. Add the peanut butter and stir until it "dissolves" and the soup is smooth.

three Reduce the heat to low, add the cayenne pepper and salt and pepper to taste, and let the mixture simmer, half covered, for 20 minutes, stirring occasionally.

four Stir in the cream and heat through, without boiling, for 1–2 minutes. Taste and adjust the seasoning, if necessary.

five Ladle the soup into warmed bowls and sprinkle over the peanuts— they will sink to the bottom, but this way they don't become soft. Sprinkle over a little chili and celery leaves and serve.

did you know?

Originally from Africa, peanuts are another now-staple ingredient introduced to the United States via the slave trade. In the South they are called goobers or goober peas, from the African word nguba, *and are primarily grown in Georgia and Virginia.*

Fried oysters are one of the most traditional fillings of this New Orleans classic. Once you choose your filling, you just have to decide if you want it "undressed" (plain) or "dressed" (with the lettuce, tomatoes, and mayonnaise).

oyster po' boys

ingredients

generous ¼ cup yellow cornmeal
⅓ cup all-purpose flour
pinch of cayenne pepper
24 fresh live oysters, shucked
vegetable oil, for deep-frying
1 French baguette, about 28 inches/
   70 cm long

hot pepper sauce, to taste (optional)
2 dill pickles, sliced (optional)
salt and pepper

dressing
mayonnaise
4 tomatoes, sliced
shredded iceberg lettuce

one Put the cornmeal, flour, cayenne pepper, and salt and pepper to taste into a plastic bag, hold closed, and shake to mix. Add the oysters and shake until well coated.

two Heat at least 2 inches/5 cm of oil in the largest skillet you have over high heat until the temperature reaches 350–375°F/180–190°C, or until a cube of bread browns in 30 seconds. Add as many oysters as will fit without overcrowding and fry for 2–3 minutes, or until the coating is crisp and lightly browned. Remove the oysters from the oil with a slotted spoon and drain on paper towels. Reheat the oil, then cook the remaining oysters.

three Cut the baguette in half, without cutting all the way through. Open the bread out like a book and use a spoon to scoop out the crumb from the bottom half, leaving a border all around the edge.

four Spread mayonnaise over the top and bottom halves. Lay the oysters all along the length. Sprinkle with hot pepper sauce to taste and dill pickles, if using. Dress with tomato slices all along the length, then add the shredded lettuce. Close the sandwich and cut into 4 equal portions and wrap in paper napkins to serve.

did you know?
The "po' boy" name supposedly came about in 1929 when two New Orleans restaurateurs took pity on striking streetcar workers and offered the "poor boys" sandwiches made from the day's leftovers. It is also nicknamed a "peacemaker" because husbands traditionally bring one home to end any marital spats.

In a country with plenty of BIG sandwiches, this New Orleans specialty is probably the biggest of all. Its distinguishing feature from other hero-style sandwiches is the piquant olive salad.

muffuletta

ingredients

1 round bread loaf, about 1 lb/450 g, with a crisp crust

3 oz/85 g smoked ham, thinly sliced

3 oz/85 g Italian mortadella or salami, thinly sliced

3 oz/85 g provolone cheese, thinly sliced

olive salad

⅓ cup pimiento-stuffed olives, thinly sliced

⅓ cup pitted black olives, thinly sliced

2 oz/55 g Italian mixed pickled vegetables (*giardiniera*), drained and chopped

2 large garlic cloves, crushed

2 tbsp chopped fresh flat-leaf parsley

½ tbsp bottled capers, drained and rinsed

½ tsp dried oregano or thyme

½ tsp Worcestershire sauce

hot pepper sauce, to taste

fruity olive oil

freshly ground black pepper

one Ideally, the olive salad is assembled a day in advance to allow the flavors to blend, but an hour or two marinating will do. Put the olives, pickled vegetables, garlic, parsley, capers, oregano, Worcestershire sauce, hot pepper sauce to taste, and black pepper into a nonmetallic bowl and add enough oil to cover with a thin layer. Stir together. Cover and let marinate at room temperature for 1–2 hours or overnight in the refrigerator.

two When ready to assemble the sandwich, cut the loaf in half horizontally and use a spoon to scoop out about ¼ inch/5 mm of the crumb from the top and bottom halves, leaving a border all around the edge. Spoon the oil from the olive salad over both halves.

three Spread about three-quarters of the salad over the bottom half of the bread. Top with the smoked ham, mortadella and, finally, the provolone cheese. Spread the remaining salad over the cheese and replace the top half of the bread. Put a heavy cutting board on top to press the sandwich together. Let stand for 1–2 hours, then cut in half or into quarters to serve.

did you know?

Central Grocery, an old-fashioned, family-run Italian deli across from New Orleans' French market, invented this sandwich, but it has been copied and changed many times. Central Grocery's muffuletta comes on a sesame-seed-topped loaf, but any firm, round loaf will do.

Most Southern cooking can be described as "home-style." Anything fancy or fussy is left for restaurant cooks to grapple with.

Chickens and pigs are cheap to keep, so they have always featured in many traditional dishes, with fried chicken being the defining dish of the South. Slow-cooked ham hocks are another inexpensive yet delicious local specialty. And the long southeastern coastline yields plentiful crab, snappers, and big-game fish for baking and broiling. Inland, catfish farms now breed tons of the once-scarce fish.

main courses

prepare 10 minutes, plus 4 hours' soaking
cook 20–40 minutes, depending on pan size *serves* 4–6

This is the signature dish of the South. Everywhere south of the Mason-Dixon line, fried chicken—golden and crisp on the outside, with tender flesh on the inside—is on the menu. Try it with mashed potato and a pot of Southern Peas.

southern fried chicken

ingredients

1 chicken, weighing 3 lb 5 oz/1.5 kg,
   cut into 6 or 8 pieces
½ cup all-purpose flour

2–4 tbsp butter
corn or peanut oil, for pan-frying
salt and pepper

one Put the chicken into a large bowl with 1 teaspoon of salt and cold water to cover, then cover the bowl and let stand in the refrigerator for at least 4 hours, but ideally overnight. Drain the chicken pieces well and pat completely dry with paper towels.

two Put the flour and salt and pepper to taste into a plastic bag, hold closed, and shake to mix. Add the chicken pieces and shake until well coated. Remove the chicken pieces from the bag and shake off any excess flour.

three Melt 2 tablespoons of the butter with about ½ inch/1 cm of oil in an ovenproof casserole or large skillet with a lid over medium-high heat.

four Add as many chicken pieces as will fit in a single layer without overcrowding, skin-side down. Cook for 5 minutes, or until the skin is golden and crisp. Turn the chicken over and cook for an additional 10–15 minutes, covered, until it is tender and the juices run clear when a skewer is inserted into the thickest part of the meat. Remove the chicken from the casserole with a slotted spoon and drain well on paper towels. Transfer to a low oven to keep warm while cooking any remaining pieces, if necessary, or let cool completely. Remove any brown bits from the dish and melt the remaining butter in the oil, adding more oil as needed, to cook the next batch.

variations

Southerners have strong opinions about how to fry chicken, and there are as many "authentic" recipes as there are Southern cooks: buttermilk can replace water for soaking; cayenne pepper, paprika, and dried thyme season the flour; cornmeal replaces the flour; bacon fat, lard, or butter are used for cooking.

prepare 20 minutes
cook about 45 minutes   *serves* 4–6

Comfortingly old-fashioned, this rich, creamy dish is easy to make. Buttermilk Biscuits or Cornsticks are typical accompaniments, but it is also good spooned over boiled rice.

creamed chicken

ingredients

4 chicken breast halves or 6 thighs
4 cups water
6 black peppercorns, lightly crushed
1 bay leaf
3 tbsp butter
1 tbsp corn or peanut oil
1 onion, finely chopped
1 red bell pepper, cored, seeded, and chopped
1 green bell pepper, cored, seeded, and chopped

2 tbsp all-purpose flour
½ tsp dried thyme
pinch of cayenne pepper, or to taste
1½ cups heavy cream
7 oz/200 g canned corn kernels, drained
2 tbsp chopped fresh parsley
salt and pepper
hot buttermilk biscuits or cornsticks, to serve

one Put the chicken and water into a large pan over medium-high heat and slowly bring to a boil, skimming the surface. When the gray foam stops rising, reduce the heat to medium, add ½ teaspoon of salt, the peppercorns, and bay leaf and let simmer for 20 minutes, or until the chicken is tender and the juices run clear when a skewer is inserted into the thickest part of the meat.

two Strain the chicken, reserving about 1¼ cups of the cooking liquid. When the chicken is cool enough to handle, remove and discard all the skin and bones and the bay leaf. Cut the flesh into bite-size pieces and set aside.

three Melt 2 tablespoons of the butter with the oil in a large skillet over medium-high heat. Add the onion and bell peppers and cook, stirring occasionally, for 5–8 minutes until they are are soft but not brown. Remove from the skillet with a slotted spoon and set aside.

four Melt the remaining butter in the pan juices. Sprinkle in the flour, thyme, cayenne pepper, and salt and pepper to taste and cook, stirring constantly, for 2 minutes. Slowly stir in the reserved cooking liquid, and continue stirring until no lumps remain. Stir in the cream and bring to a boil. Boil until the sauce is reduced by about half.

five Reduce the heat to medium. Stir the chicken into the skillet with the corn, bell peppers, and onion and heat through. Stir in the parsley and adjust the seasoning, if necessary. Serve spooned over hot buttermilk biscuits or with cornsticks on the side.

prepare 10 minutes
cook 10–15 minutes, depending on pan size serves 4

This quick dish with its creamy sauce is prepared for breakfast, lunch, or dinner throughout the Southern states. For breakfast, try it with hash-browns or pan-fried potatoes, but later in the day, mashed potatoes and green beans are the usual accompaniments.

chicken-fried steak with country gravy

ingredients

4 round steaks, about 5 oz/140 g each
1 cup all-purpose flour
pinch of cayenne pepper, or to taste

3–4 tbsp rendered bacon fat or
  corn or peanut oil
1¼ cups milk or light cream
salt and pepper

one Put the steaks between pieces of waxed paper and use a rolling pin to beat them until they are about ¼ inch/5 mm thick. Set aside.

two Put the flour onto a large plate and season with cayenne pepper and salt and pepper to taste. Dust the steaks with the seasoned flour on both sides, shaking off any excess, and set aside the leftover flour.

three Heat 3 tablespoons of the bacon fat in a large skillet over medium-high heat. Add as many steaks as will fit without overcrowding the skillet and cook for 5–6 minutes, turning once, until they are cooked through as desired and are crisp and brown on the outside. Transfer the steaks to a plate and keep warm in a low oven while cooking the remaining steaks, if necessary. Add more fat to the skillet as needed.

four To make the country gravy, put 5 tablespoons of the reserved seasoned flour into a small bowl, slowly stir in half the milk, and continue stirring until no lumps remain.

five Pour off all but about 1 tablespoon of the fat in the skillet. Pour the milk mixture into the skillet, stirring to scrape up the sediment. Pour in the remaining milk and bring to a boil. Reduce the heat and let simmer for 2 minutes, stirring constantly, to remove the raw flour taste. Taste and adjust the seasoning, if necessary. Serve the steaks with the gravy poured over.

did you know?
The Southern term "chicken-fried" refers to cooking inexpensive cuts of steak as if they were chicken in a seasoned-flour coating. (Southern cooks also cook green tomatoes this way.) Chicken-fried steak first appeared on Southern menus in the 1950s. Sometimes it is also listed as "smothered steak" or "country-fried steak."

prepare 15 minutes
cook 2¾–3¼ hours serves 4–6

For most Americans, this simple one-pot dish captures the essence of Southern soul food. The choice of greens is not that important—the distinctive flavor comes from using smoked ham hocks.

ham hocks
with greens

ingredients

2 large, meaty, smoked ham hocks,
 weighing 2 lb 12 oz/1.25 kg each
2 lb 12 oz/1.25 kg collard or other greens

2 onions, chopped
½ tsp dried red pepper flakes, or to taste
salt and pepper

one Put the ham hocks into a large, deep flameproof casserole with enough water to cover over high heat. Bring the water to a boil, skimming the surface. Reduce the heat to medium-low and let the knuckles simmer, covered, for 2 hours, or until the meat starts to feel tender when you prod it with a knife.

two Meanwhile, rinse the greens in several changes of water to remove all grit and dirt. Supermarket greens will probably require less rinsing, but any greens bought at a farmers' market must be carefully rinsed. Cut out and discard any thick stems and slice the greens. Set aside.

three Drain the ham hocks and return them to the casserole with the onions and pepper flakes. Add enough fresh water to cover the ham hocks.

four Cover and bring the water to a boil, then reduce the heat, uncover, and stir in the greens. Let simmer, uncovered, for 30 minutes–1 hour, or until the greens and ham hocks are both tender. Check the greens for tenderness periodically, as some cook much more quickly than others.

five Remove the ham hocks from the casserole and cut the meat from the bones, discarding the skin and excess fat. Cut the meat into bite-size pieces. Taste the greens and add salt and pepper to taste. Transfer the greens to a warmed serving plate using a slotted spoon. Top with the pieces of ham. The dish can be served as it is, or with a little of the "pot likker" (as the cooking liquid is described in old recipes) spooned over.

did you know?

It is ironic that this dish is now served in fashionable restaurants. For generations of rural poor, greens represented one of the cheapest sources of food. Collard, with their especially bitter flavor, were shunned by wealthy landowners and left for slaves and plantation workers.

prepare 15 minutes, plus 8 hours' marinating
cook 1½–2 hours *serves* 4–6

It wouldn't be Fourth of July in the South without a barbecue. For many, the phrase "come to a barbecue" means cooking a whole hog in a pit, but this recipe is more suited to a home "cookout."

barbecue rack of ribs

ingredients

2 racks of pork ribs,
  about 1 lb 7 oz/650 g each
vegetable oil, for brushing

tennessee rub
1 tbsp ground cumin
1 tsp garlic salt
½ tsp ground cinnamon
½ tsp dry English mustard powder
½ tsp ground coriander
1 tsp dried mixed herbs
⅛ tsp cayenne pepper, or to taste

bourbon barbecue sauce
1 tbsp corn or peanut oil
½ onion, finely chopped
2 large garlic cloves, minced
generous ⅓ cup packed brown sugar
1 tbsp dry English mustard powder
1 tsp ground cumin
2 tbsp tomato paste
6 tbsp bourbon
2 tbsp Worcestershire sauce
2 tbsp apple or white wine vinegar
few drops of hot pepper sauce, to taste

one A day ahead, mix all the ingredients for the rub together in a small bowl. Rub the mixture onto both sides of the ribs, then cover and let them marinate in the refrigerator overnight.

two To make the barbecue sauce, heat the oil in a pan over medium-high heat. Add the onion and garlic and cook for 5 minutes, stirring frequently, or until the onion is soft. Stir in the remaining sauce ingredients. Slowly bring to a boil, stirring to dissolve the sugar, then reduce the heat and let simmer, uncovered, for 30 minutes–1 hour, stirring occasionally, until dark brown and very thick. Let cool, then cover and let chill until required.

three When ready to barbecue, heat the coals until they are glowing. Brush the barbecue rack with a little oil. Put the ribs onto the rack and cook, turning frequently, for 40 minutes, or until the meat feels tender. If they appear to be drying out, brush with water.

four Remove the ribs from the barbecue and cut them into 1- or 2-rib portions. Return the rib portions to the barbecue and brush with the sauce. Cook the ribs, turning frequently and basting generously with the sauce, for an additional 10 minutes, or until they are dark brown and glossy. Serve with a bowl of the hot leftover sauce for dipping—and plenty of paper napkins for sticky fingers!

prepare about 20 minutes
cook about 2¼ hours *serves* 4–6

A cross between a soup and a stew, gumbo is one of the great dishes of Louisiana Creole cooking. All gumbos begin with the essential slowly cooked roux, and are then thickened with okra or filé.

chicken gumbo

ingredients

1 chicken, weighing 3 lb 5 oz/1.5 kg, cut into 6 pieces
2 celery stalks, 1 broken in half and 1 finely chopped
1 carrot, peeled and chopped
2 onions, 1 sliced and 1 chopped
1 bay leaf
4 tbsp corn or peanut oil
⅓ cup all-purpose flour
2 large garlic cloves, crushed
1 green bell pepper, cored, seeded, and diced
1 lb/450 g fresh okra, trimmed, then cut crosswise into ½-inch/ 1-cm slices

8 oz/225 g andouille sausage or Polish kielbasa, sliced
2 tbsp tomato paste
1 bay leaf
1 tsp dried thyme
½ tsp salt
½ tsp cayenne pepper
¼ tsp pepper
14 oz/400 g canned peeled plum tomatoes
salt

to serve
cooked long-grain white rice
hot pepper sauce

one Put the chicken into a large pan with water to cover over medium-high heat and bring to a boil, skimming the surface. When the foam stops rising, reduce the heat to medium, add the celery stalk halves, carrot, sliced onion, bay leaf, and ¼ teaspoon of salt and let simmer for 20 minutes, or until the chicken is tender and the juices run clear when a skewer is inserted into the thickest part of the meat. Strain the chicken, reserving 4 cups of the liquid. When the chicken is cool enough to handle, remove and discard all the skin, bones, and flavorings. Cut the flesh into bite-size pieces and set aside.

two Heat the oil in a large pan over medium-high heat for 2 minutes. Reduce the heat to low, sprinkle in the flour, and stir to make the roux. Stir constantly for 30 minutes, or until the roux turns a hazelnut-brown color. If black specks appear, it is burned and you will have to start again.

three Add the chopped celery, chopped onion, garlic, bell pepper, and okra to the pan. Increase the heat to medium-high and cook, stirring frequently, for 5 minutes. Add the sausage and cook, stirring frequently, for 2 minutes.

four Stir in the remaining ingredients and the reserved cooking liquid. Bring to a boil, crushing the tomatoes with a wooden spoon. Reduce the heat to medium-low and let simmer, uncovered, for 30 minutes, stirring occasionally.

five Add the chicken to the pan and let simmer for an additional 30 minutes. Taste and adjust the seasoning, if necessary. Spoon the gumbo over the rice and serve with a bottle of hot pepper sauce on the side.

Early Colonial cookbooks used opossum, raccoon, or squirrel in this stew. Usually made to feed a large number, it was originally simmered over a fire in a large pot until the bones rose to the top.

brunswick stew

ingredients

1 chicken, weighing 3 lb 5 oz/1.5 kg, cut into 6 pieces

1 rabbit, dressed, skinned, and chopped

1 bay leaf

2 tbsp corn oil

2 large onions, finely chopped

1 large celery stalk, strings removed, finely chopped

1 lb/450 g juicy, ripe tomatoes, peeled, seeded, and chopped

2 tbsp tomato paste

1 tbsp dried thyme

½ tbsp Worcestershire sauce

¼ tsp cayenne pepper, or to taste

1 lb/450 g potatoes, peeled and diced

2 large corn ears, kernels cut off

2 cups shelled fava beans

salt and pepper

chopped fresh parsley, to garnish

one Put the chicken and rabbit into a large pan with water to cover by 2 inches/5 cm over high heat. Bring to a boil, skimming the surface. Reduce the heat, add the bay leaf, and 2 teaspoons of salt and let simmer for 1 hour, or until both meats are tender and starting to fall off the bones.

two Meanwhile, heat the oil in a large, flameproof casserole over medium heat. Add the onions and celery and cook, stirring frequently, for 3–5 minutes until soft, but not browned. Set aside until the chicken and rabbit are cooked.

three Remove the chicken and rabbit pieces from the cooking liquid with a slotted spoon. When cool enough to handle, remove and discard all the skin and bones. Cut the flesh into large bite-size pieces and set aside. Pour 5 cups of the cooking liquid into the casserole. Stir in the tomatoes, tomato paste, thyme, Worcestershire sauce, cayenne pepper, and salt and pepper to taste, bring to a boil, and boil for 2 minutes. Reduce the heat, add the potatoes, corn kernels, and fava beans, and let simmer for 20 minutes, or until the potatoes are tender but not falling apart.

four Return the chicken and rabbit to the stew and heat through. Taste and adjust the seasoning, if necessary. Sprinkle with parsley and serve.

did you know?

One of the great food rivalries in the United States rages between Brunswick, Georgia, and Brunswick County, Virginia—both claim to be the home of this Southern specialty. Differences are subtle and many, but chicken replaces some of the wild meat in modern versions, such as this chicken/rabbit combination.

prepare 20 minutes
cook about 35 minutes   *serves* 4

Warm waters in the Gulf of Mexico are ideal for red snapper, making it a popular fish with fishermen and cooks alike. This recipe teams the snapper's tender, mild flesh with fresh orange juice.

stuffed red snapper

ingredients

1 red snapper, weighing 2 lb 4 oz/1 kg, cleaned and scaled, then rinsed and patted dry
lemon or orange wedges, to serve

orange basting sauce
generous ¼ cup corn oil
2 tbsp butter, melted
3 tbsp freshly squeezed orange juice
2 tbsp Worcestershire sauce
hot pepper sauce, to taste
salt and pepper

citrus-shrimp stuffing
2 tbsp butter or 2 tbsp corn oil
2 tbsp red onion, very finely chopped
1 celery stalk, strings removed, minced
½ cup fine dried white bread crumbs
3 oz/85 g cooked shelled shrimp, chopped
1½ oz/40 g cooked fresh crabmeat, picked over, or thawed and patted dry if frozen
2 tbsp chopped fresh parsley
½ tsp dried thyme or tarragon
finely grated rind and juice of 1 large orange

one Preheat the oven to 350°F/180°C. To make the basting sauce, put all the ingredients into a screw-top jar and shake until blended. Set aside.

two To make the stuffing, melt the butter in a skillet over medium heat. Add the onion and celery and cook, stirring frequently, for 3–5 minutes until they are soft but not brown. Stir in the bread crumbs, shrimp, crabmeat, parsley, thyme, and orange rind. Slowly stir in the orange juice just until the stuffing is well blended. Add salt and pepper to taste.

three Season the red snapper's cavity with salt and pepper. Spoon in the stuffing and use wooden toothpicks to close the cavity and hold the stuffing in. Lay the fish in a roasting pan and pour over the basting sauce. Bake in the oven, basting once or twice, for 30 minutes, or until the fish is cooked through and the flesh flakes easily. Let rest for 2–3 minutes, then transfer the fish to a warmed serving platter, with lemon wedges for squeezing over.

cook's tip
Red snapper, also called Florida snapper, is easy to spot on the fish counter—it is dark red on top, fading to a more rosy red at the belly, with a silver sheen. If you can't find red snapper, this citrus-flavored stuffing also works well with sea bass.

Swordfish is a big-game fish caught in the Atlantic Ocean all along the Southern east coast. Its firm, meaty flesh responds well to being treated like a steak, as here with a savory butter. This recipe has the flavors of Miami's Cuban neighborhoods.

broiled swordfish with cilantro-lime butter

ingredients

corn oil, for brushing
4 swordfish steaks, about 6 oz/
   175 g each and 1 inch/2.5 cm thick
salt and pepper
fresh cilantro leaves, to garnish

cilantro-lime butter
4½ oz/125 g unsalted butter, softened
finely grated rind of 1 large lime
¼ tsp freshly squeezed lime juice
1 tbsp very finely shredded
   cilantro leaves
pinch of ground cumin

one To make the cilantro-lime butter, put the butter into a bowl and beat until it is soft and smooth. Stir in the lime rind, lime juice, shredded cilantro, cumin, and salt and pepper to taste. Spoon the butter onto a piece of waxed paper and roll into a log about 1¼ inches/3 cm thick. Refrigerate for at least 45 minutes or freeze until required.

two When ready to cook the swordfish steaks, preheat the broiler to high. Brush the broiler rack with a little oil and position it about 4 inches/10 cm below the heat source.

three Brush the steaks with oil and season to taste with salt and pepper. Put the steaks onto the broiler rack and cook for 4 minutes. Turn them over, then brush with a little more oil, season to taste with salt and pepper, and cook for an additional 4–5 minutes, or until cooked and the flesh flakes easily.

four Meanwhile, cut the butter into 8 equal slices. Put 2 slices of the butter on top of each steak and serve at once, garnished with cilantro leaves.

variation
Swordfish steaks are also good when cooked on the barbecue. The barbecue coals are ready to use when you can hold your hand over the rack for only 3–4 seconds.

prepare 10 minutes
cook 4–8 minutes, depending on pan size   *serves* 4

When Southerners talk about "fried fish," the chances are it's catfish, a bottom-feeding freshwater fish, they are referring to. Small, makeshift-looking restaurants all along the Mississippi River pan-fry catfish with a crispy cornmeal coating.

fried catfish fillets

ingredients

½ cup all-purpose flour
2 eggs
1½ cups yellow cornmeal
½ tsp dried thyme
pinch of cayenne pepper
corn oil, for pan-frying

2 lb/900 g catfish fillets, skinned, rinsed,
  and patted dry
salt and pepper

to serve
hush puppies
coleslaw
lemon wedges

one Put the flour onto a plate. Beat the eggs in a wide, shallow bowl. Put the cornmeal onto a separate plate and season with the thyme, cayenne pepper, and salt and pepper to taste.

two Dust the catfish fillets with the seasoned flour on both sides, shaking off any excess, dip into the eggs, then pat the cornmeal onto both sides.

three Heat about 2 inches/5 cm of oil in a large skillet over medium heat. Add as many catfish fillets as will fit without overcrowding the skillet and cook for 2 minutes, or until the coating is golden brown.

four Turn the catfish fillets over and cook for an additional 2 minutes, or until the flesh flakes easily. Remove from the skillet with a slotted spoon and drain on paper towels. Transfer the fillets to a low oven to keep warm while cooking the remaining fillets, if necessary. Add more oil to the skillet as needed.

five For a true Southern meal, serve the fried catfish with hush puppies and coleslaw. French fries are another popular accompaniment.

variation

Not many years ago, catfish was rarely available outside the South, and was an acquired taste. But now, catfish farming is big business in Mississippi, Louisiana, and Alabama, so catfish is widely available and with less of a "muddy" taste. If you can't find any catfish, substitute river trout fillets.

prepare 15 minutes, plus 1¼ hours' chilling
cook 6–12 minutes, depending on pan size *makes* 8

Virginia cooks along the Chesapeake Bay and Atlantic coast are renowned for their light, delicate crab cakes pan-fried in butter. Only a small amount of mayonnaise binds the ingredients, so allow plenty of chilling time, which makes handling easier.

chesapeake crab cakes

ingredients

3 eggs

2 scallions, finely chopped

3 tbsp mayonnaise

1 tbsp Dijon mustard

1 tbsp bottled grated horseradish

1 tbsp bottled capers, rinsed, drained, and chopped

1 tbsp chopped fresh parsley

½ tsp salt

¼ tsp pepper

pinch of cayenne pepper, or to taste

1 lb/450 g cooked fresh crabmeat, picked over, or thawed and patted dry if frozen

½ cup milk

½ cup all-purpose flour

2 cups fine dried white bread crumbs

up to 2 oz/55 g butter, for pan-frying

corn oil, for pan-frying

lime wedges, to serve

one Combine one of the eggs, the scallions, mayonnaise, mustard, horseradish, capers, parsley, salt, pepper, and cayenne pepper in a bowl and beat together. Stir in the crabmeat, then cover and chill for at least 30 minutes.

two Meanwhile, beat the remaining eggs with the milk in a wide, shallow bowl. Put the flour and bread crumbs onto separate plates. With wet hands, shape the crabmeat mixture into 8 equal balls and form into patties about 1 inch/2.5 cm thick. If the crab cakes feel too soft to hold their shape, return them to the refrigerator for 15 minutes, otherwise proceed with the next step.

three Lightly dust a crab cake with flour on both sides. Dip into the egg mixture, then pat the bread crumbs onto both sides. Continue until all the crab cakes are coated. Cover them and let chill for at least 45 minutes.

four Melt 2 tablespoons of the butter with ½ inch/1 cm of oil in a large skillet over medium heat. Add as many crab cakes as will fit without overcrowding the skillet and cook for 3 minutes on each side until golden brown and crisp.

five Remove the crab cakes from the skillet with a slotted spoon and drain on paper towels. Transfer to a low oven to keep warm while cooking the remaining crab cakes. Add more butter and oil to the skillet as needed.

It's a Southern tradition to invite friends and family in for a bowl of hoppin' john on New Year's Day. Legend maintains that the more black-eye peas you eat, the more prosperous the year will be. Whereas, without a bowl of hoppin' john, only bad luck will follow.

hoppin' john

ingredients

1 unsmoked ham hock, weighing
  2 lb 12 oz/1.25 kg
1 cup dried black-eye peas, soaked
  overnight in water to cover
2 large celery stalks, broken in half and
  tied together with a bay leaf
1 large onion, chopped

1 dried red chili (optional)
1 tbsp rendered bacon fat or corn or
  peanut oil
1 cup Carolina long-grain rice
salt and pepper
hot pepper sauce, to serve

one Put the ham hock into a large, flameproof casserole with water to cover over high heat. Bring to a boil, skimming the surface. Cover, reduce the heat, and let simmer for 1½ hours.

two Stir in the peas, celery bundle, onion, and chili, if using, and let simmer for an additional 1½–2 hours, or until the peas are tender but not mushy and the ham hock feels tender when you prod it with a knife.

three Strain the "pot likker" (as the cooking liquid is described in old recipes) into a large bowl and reserve. Set the ham hock aside and set the peas aside separately, removing and discarding the flavorings.

four Heat the bacon fat in a pan or flameproof casserole with a tight-fitting lid over medium heat. Add the rice and stir until coated with the fat. Stir in 2 cups of the reserved cooking liquid, the peas, and salt and pepper to taste. (Use the remaining cooking liquid for soup or discard.) Bring to a boil, stirring constantly, then reduce the heat to very low, cover, and let simmer for 20 minutes without lifting the lid.

five Meanwhile, cut the meat from the ham hock, discarding the skin and excess fat. Cut the meat into bite-size pieces.

six Remove the pan from the heat and let stand for 5 minutes, again without lifting the lid. Fluff up the rice and peas with a fork and stir in the ham, then pile onto a warmed serving platter. Serve with a bottle of hot pepper sauce on the side. Traditional accompaniments include boiled greens and cornbread.

One satisfying feature of dining in the South is the variety of side dishes always on offer. Cooks think nothing of producing buttermilk biscuits or cornbread at a moment's notice—both delicious served piping hot with butter. Other corn-based specialties include Spoon Bread, Hush Puppies, and Baked Grits with Cheese.

Fried okra and black-eye peas come from the tradition of soul-food cooking, and no barbecue would ever be complete without Coleslaw. Macaroni and Cheese and Dirty Rice are renowned Creole favorites from Louisiana.

on the side

There is no higher accolade for a Southern cook than praising the flakiness of his or her biscuits. Making biscuits is second nature to traditional Southern cooks, as many Southerners don't consider a breakfast, lunch, or dinner complete without hot biscuits.

buttermilk biscuits

ingredients

1¾ cups all-purpose flour, plus extra
  for dusting
1 tbsp superfine sugar
2 tsp baking powder
½ tsp salt
½ tsp baking soda

4 tbsp butter or half butter and half
  white vegetable fat, diced
⅔ cup buttermilk, plus 1–2 tbsp if
  needed
a little milk, to glaze
butter, to serve

one Preheat the oven to 425°F/220°C. Lightly dust a baking sheet with flour.

two Sift the flour, sugar, baking powder, salt, and baking soda into a bowl.

three Add the butter, and rub in with the fingertips until coarse crumbs form. Stir in the ⅔ cup of buttermilk and quickly mix into a moist dough with a fork. If dry ingredients remain in the bottom of the bowl, add the extra buttermilk, 1 tablespoon at a time, but do not overmix or the biscuits will be heavy.

four Turn the dough out onto a lightly floured counter and very lightly pat out until ¾ inch/2 cm thick. Use a floured 2½-inch/6-cm biscuit or cookie cutter to stamp out 6–7 biscuits, lightly rerolling the trimmings as necessary. To help the biscuits rise while baking, press straight down with the cutter and do not twist it.

five Put the biscuits onto the prepared baking sheet and lightly brush the tops with a little milk to glaze. Use the tines of a fork to prick the top of each biscuit in several places.

six Bake the biscuits in the oven for 15 minutes, or until they are risen and golden brown on top. Serve at once with plenty of butter.

did you know?
Buttermilk biscuits are one of the best examples of American quick breads—leavened baked goods that are quick to mix and bake, similar to Irish soda bread. For generations, Southern households have woken to the aroma of fresh baking without the cook having had to rise hours earlier to make fresh bread dough.

prepare 10 minutes, plus 15 minutes' cooling
cook 40–45 minutes *serves* 4–6

The word "bread" in the title of this Southern classic is a misnomer, as the texture is more like a cornmeal soufflé or pudding. Its name might be derived from the Native American word for porridge, *suppawn*, or simply because it is served with a spoon, straight from the baking dish.

spoon bread

ingredients

2 cups yellow cornmeal

1½ tsp salt

2 tbsp butter, plus extra for greasing and to serve (optional)

2½ cups boiling water

2 eggs, separated

1 tsp baking soda

1½ cups buttermilk

one Preheat the oven to 425°F/220°C. Grease a 1½-quart baking dish suitable for serving from.

two Stir the cornmeal and salt together in a heatproof bowl. Add the butter and boiling water and stir until the mixture is smooth, then set it aside to cool slightly.

three Stir the egg yolks into the cornmeal mixture. Stir the baking soda into the buttermilk in a pitcher until dissolved, then stir into the cornmeal mixture to make a thin, smooth batter.

four Using an electric mixer, beat the egg whites in a separate bowl until stiff peaks form. Beat a large spoonful of the egg whites into the cornmeal batter to lighten, then fold in the remainder.

five Spoon the batter into the prepared dish and bake in the oven for 40–45 minutes, or until the top is set and golden brown. Serve straight from the dish while the spoon bread is hot, with plenty of butter to melt over the top of each portion.

did you know?

Southern cooks prefer to make spoon bread with white cornmeal, but as it is rarely sold outside the region, yellow cornmeal is used in most recipes. In Colonial days, spoon bread took the place of bread made with refined white flour, which was prohibitively expensive for all but the wealthiest.

Golden yellow cornbread is popular throughout the South, and one tradition is to bake it in cast-iron cornstick molds, producing single portions that look like ears of corn. These cornsticks can be served hot or cold and are a natural partner for Southern Fried Chicken.

cornsticks

ingredients

corn oil, for oiling
scant 1¼ cups yellow cornmeal
¾ cup all-purpose flour, sifted
1½–2 tbsp superfine sugar, to taste
2½ tsp baking powder
¾ tsp salt

5 scallions, finely chopped
generous 1 cup milk
1 egg
3 tbsp butter, melted, plus extra
  to serve

one Preheat the oven to 425°F/220°C. Generously brush two 7-stick molds with oil and place them in the oven while it heats.

two Do not start mixing the cornmeal batter until the oven has reached the correct temperature. Stir the cornmeal, flour, sugar, baking powder, and salt together in a bowl, then stir in the scallions. Make a well in the center.

three Mix the milk, egg, and butter together in a pitcher, then stir into the dry ingredients until just mixed. Do not overmix.

four Remove the hot molds from the oven and divide the cornmeal batter between them, filling each mold about three-quarters full. Return the molds to the oven and bake for 20–25 minutes, or until each cornstick is risen and coming away from the side of the mold. A wooden toothpick inserted into the center should come out clean.

five Let the cornsticks stand for 1 minute, then use a round-bladed knife to ease them out of the molds. Serve at once with butter for spreading over the cornsticks.

cook's tip
If you don't have cornstick molds, this mixture can also be baked in a 9-inch/23-cm square baking dish or a large cast-iron skillet. Cornbread is best served hot, straight from the oven, but any leftovers can be wrapped in foil and reheated in the oven at 350°F/180°C for 10–15 minutes.

Stewed tomatoes are a traditional Southern side dish, again with many variations. This sweet, baked recipe, with bread cubes to soak up the moisture of the tomatoes as they cook, is good for entertaining, as it can be assembled in advance and baked at the last minute.

scalloped tomatoes

ingredients

1 lb 5 oz/600 g juicy, ripe tomatoes, coarsely chopped
3½ oz/100 g fresh bread, cut into ¼-inch/5-mm cubes
4 scallions, finely chopped

1 tbsp tomato paste (optional)
4 tbsp butter, diced
⅓ cup packed brown sugar
chopped fresh parsley or snipped chives, to garnish

one Preheat the oven to 400°F/200°C. Put the tomatoes, bread cubes, and scallions into a baking dish and gently toss together. If the tomatoes are not bright red, stir in the tomato paste.

two Scatter the diced butter over the surface and sprinkle with the sugar. Bake in the oven for 15 minutes. Give the tomatoes a good stir then bake for an additional 15 minutes.

three Increase the temperature to 425°F/220°C. Give the tomatoes a final stir and bake for an additional 10 minutes, or until the tomatoes are tender and the bread cubes are slightly caramelized. Sprinkle with the parsley and serve hot.

did you know?
Scalloped tomatoes have been a part of Southern dining for several hundred years. Preserved menus reveal that Thomas Jefferson served them in the splendid meals at Monticello, his plantation on the banks of the Potomac River, in the late 18th century.

Most Americans eat sweet potatoes just once a year with their Thanksgiving turkey, but for Southerners, these orange-fleshed tubers are a more versatile everyday vegetable.

candied
sweet potatoes

ingredients

3 large orange-fleshed sweet potatoes, about 9 oz/250 g each, scrubbed

2 tbsp butter, melted and cooled, plus extra for greasing

¼ cup packed brown sugar

finely grated rind of ½ orange

4 tbsp freshly squeezed orange juice

pinch of cayenne pepper, or to taste (optional)

one Bring a large pan of water to a boil over high heat. Add the sweet potatoes and cook for 15 minutes. Drain, then put them under cold running water to cool. When cool enough to handle, peel, then cut each into 8 wedges or chunks. Spread out in the prepared baking dish.

two Meanwhile, preheat the oven to 400°F/200°C. Lightly grease a baking dish large enough to hold all the wedges or chunks in a single layer.

three Put the butter, sugar, and orange rind and juice into a small pan over medium heat and stir until the sugar dissolves. Bring to a boil and boil until the liquid reduces by about one-third. Stir in the cayenne pepper, if using.

four Generously brush the sweet potatoes with the glaze. Bake in the oven, glazing an additional 2–3 times at intervals, for 20–30 minutes, or until the sweet potatoes are tender when pierced with the tip of a knife or a skewer. These are excellent served hot, or left to cool and served as part of a picnic or barbecue spread.

cook's tip

Two varieties of sweet potato (Ipomoea batatas) are grown in the South—one with a pale yellow flesh and the other with a vibrant orange flesh. It is the orange-fleshed variety that you need for this dish. These are often referred to as "yams" by Southerners, but true yams (Dioscorea bulbifera) are quite different.

Along with hush puppies, this is an essential side dish for a pan-fried catfish meal. Some recipes are made with mayonnaise, but this version is less cloying. It also goes well with barbecued ribs and Southern fried chicken.

coleslaw

ingredients

8 oz/225 g white cabbage,
  cored and grated

8 oz/225 g carrots, peeled and grated

4 tbsp sugar

3 tbsp cider vinegar

½ cup heavy cream, lightly whipped

2 pickled green or red bell peppers,
  drained and thinly sliced (optional)

4 tbsp finely chopped fresh parsley

salt and pepper

one Combine the cabbage, carrots, sugar, vinegar, a large pinch of salt, and pepper to taste in a large bowl, tossing the ingredients together. Cover and let chill for 1 hour.

two Stir all the ingredients together well. Lightly stir in the whipped cream and the pickled bell peppers, if using. Taste and add extra sugar, vinegar, or salt, if desired. Sprinkle over the parsley and serve at once. Alternatively, cover and let chill until required.

did you know?

Coleslaw isn't exclusive to the South—every region of America has a version of this creamy, crunchy salad—but it has been a part of Southern culinary history since European settlers arrived. One of the earliest Southern versions is recorded in the Kentucky Housewife, *published by Lettice Bryan in 1839.*

Grits, made from ground dried corn kernels that have been soaked in a water-lye solution, are rarely eaten in other parts of the country, but Southerners eat them at any time of the day—especially for breakfast, served like oatmeal with salt and melting butter.

baked grits
with **cheese**

ingredients

3 cups water	½ tsp salt
1 cup "instant" grits	2 pickled green bell peppers, drained
2 eggs, lightly beaten	and sliced (optional)
3½ oz/100 g butter, diced, plus extra	9 oz/250 g sharp Cheddar cheese,
for greasing	coarsely grated

one Preheat the oven to 350°F/180°C. Lightly grease a 9-inch/23-cm square baking dish.

two Bring the water to a boil in a pan over high heat and sprinkle in the grits. Reduce the heat to medium and cook, stirring constantly, until a thick "mush" forms.

three Remove the pan from the heat and stir in the eggs, butter, salt, peppers, if using, and 1 cup of the cheese, beating until the butter melts and the ingredients are blended.

four Spoon the grit mixture into the prepared baking dish and smooth the top. Sprinkle over the remaining cheese. Bake in the oven for 1 hour, or until the mixture is set and the top is golden brown and bubbling.

five Any leftover baked grits can be pan-fried the following morning for breakfast. Heat a thin layer of bacon fat or corn oil in a skillet and cut the leftover grits into strips or squares. Fry the grit strips or squares for 2–3 minutes on each side until golden brown.

cook's tip

This side dish uses "instant" grits. If you can find only "quick-cooking" grits, they will have to simmer for about 5 minutes in Step 2. Older, traditional recipes feature stone-ground grits, but these modern varieties are most readily available.

prepare 10 minutes
cook about 10 minutes *serves* 4–6

Most Americans claim indifference to or dislike of okra, but in the South, this long, green, ridged pod is the star of many traditional soul-food recipes, as well as Creole and Cajun dishes. This is the recipe to win over anyone who doesn't like cooked okra's texture.

deep-fried okra

ingredients

1 lb/450 g fresh okra, trimmed and cut into ½-inch/1-cm thick slices
about 4 tbsp water
½ cup yellow cornmeal

3 tbsp self-rising or all-purpose flour
½ tsp salt
pepper
vegetable oil, for deep-frying

one Put the okra into a bowl, sprinkle over the water, and gently stir the okra, to just moisten.

two Put the cornmeal, flour, salt, and pepper to taste into a plastic bag, hold closed, and shake to mix. Add the okra slices to the bag and shake until lightly coated—they won't become completely coated.

three Heat at least 2 inches/5 cm of oil in a deep skillet or pan over high heat until the temperature reaches 350–375°F/180–190°C, or until a cube of bread browns in 30 seconds. Add as many okra slices as will fit without overcrowding the skillet and cook, stirring occasionally, for 2 minutes, or until the okra is bright green and the cornmeal coating is golden yellow.

four Remove the okra from the oil with a slotted spoon and drain on paper towels. Reheat the oil, if necessary, and cook the remaining okra.

five Serve the okra slices hot as a side dish with roast poultry, seafood, or meat, or with spoon bread. Alternatively, serve hot or cold as a snack.

cook's tip

Originally from Africa, okra is now grown throughout the region, with Georgia, Florida, and Texas growers supplying most of the nation. Okra's most distinctive characteristic is the slimy substance it gives off when cut and heated; it's used to thicken soups and stews. This deep-frying technique, however, keeps it crunchy.

Black-eye peas—small, nut-brown, kidney-shaped peas with a black "eye"—are used in many soul-food and Cajun recipes. For a true taste of the Deep South, serve these as an accompaniment to broiled ribs or meat, with simmered greens and Cornsticks.

a pot of
southern peas

ingredients

8 oz/225 g boneless, rindless belly of
  pork, cut into ½-inch/1-cm strips
2 large garlic cloves, crushed
1 onion, finely chopped
1 red bell pepper, cored, seeded, and
  finely chopped
1 celery stalk, strings removed,
  finely chopped
1 fresh red chili, seeded and chopped

4 large tomatoes, peeled, seeded,
  and chopped
1 cup water
1 lb 12 oz/800 g canned black-eye peas,
  drained and rinsed
1 tbsp blackstrap molasses
salt and pepper
hot pepper sauce, to serve

one Put the belly of pork into a deep, dry skillet or pan with a lid over medium-high heat and cook, stirring occasionally, for 10–15 minutes, or until brown and crisp. Remove the pork from the skillet with a slotted spoon and set aside. Pour off all but 1½–2 tablespoons of the rendered fat.

two Reduce the heat to medium, stir in the garlic and onion and cook, stirring frequently, for 3–5 minutes, or until the onion is soft. Add the bell pepper, celery, and chili and cook, stirring occasionally, for an additional 3 minutes. Add the tomatoes, water, and pepper to taste and bring to a boil. Reduce the heat, cover, and let simmer for 20 minutes.

three Return the pork to the skillet with the peas and molasses and stir to dissolve the molasses. Uncover the skillet and let the beans simmer, stirring occasionally, for 10 minutes, or until most of the liquid has evaporated and the beans are hot. Season to taste and serve with a bottle of hot pepper sauce on the side.

did you know?

Black-eye peas, called cowpeas in the South, are another staple ingredient brought from Africa via the slave trade. It is a long-standing Southern tradition to eat black-eye peas on New Year's Day in hoppin' john.

Don't let the title of this Cajun dish from the Louisiana backwaters put you off—"dirty" refers to the dusty brown color of the rice combined with stewed chicken livers.

dirty rice

ingredients

2 tbsp rendered bacon fat or corn oil

2 tbsp all-purpose flour

2 large garlic cloves, very finely chopped

1 onion, finely chopped

1 celery stalk, strings removed, finely chopped

½ green bell pepper, cored, seeded, and finely chopped

4 tbsp finely chopped fresh parsley

1 lb/450 g chicken livers, thawed if frozen, trimmed, and chopped

½ tsp Worcestershire sauce

pinch of cayenne pepper, or to taste

½ cup chicken or vegetable stock

1 cup long-grain rice

6 scallions, finely chopped

salt and pepper

hot pepper sauce, to serve

one Heat the bacon fat in a large skillet over medium-high heat for 1–2 minutes. Reduce the heat to medium-low, sprinkle in the flour, and stir to make a smooth paste, or roux. Stir constantly for 20 minutes, or until the roux turns a golden brown color.

two Stir in the garlic, onion, celery, bell pepper, and parsley and cook, stirring frequently, for 2–3 minutes, or until the vegetables are softened. Add the chicken livers, Worcestershire sauce, cayenne pepper, and salt and pepper to taste and cook, stirring constantly with a wooden spoon to break down the livers, for 5 minutes.

three Add the stock and bring to a boil, stirring constantly. Reduce the heat to low and let simmer, uncovered, for 15 minutes, stirring occasionally.

four Meanwhile, cook the rice in a pan of lightly salted boiling water until it is light and fluffy. Drain well and keep warm until the chicken livers and vegetables are cooked.

five Stir the rice and scallions into the liver mixture and adjust the seasoning. Serve at once, with a bottle of hot pepper sauce on the side.

did you know?

Cajun cooking is country cooking, unlike the more refined Creole cooking of the cities. Cajun cooks, generally poor and thrifty, were creative at using every part of an animal, and traditional recipes for this dish include chicken gizzards as well as livers.

When you order a meal at informal restaurants in the South, it's not unusual for main courses to come with a choice of two side dishes, and this dish is always an option. Southern cooks give this all-American favorite a regional twist by including pickled chili peppers.

macaroni & cheese

ingredients

1½ cups dried elbow macaroni

4 tbsp butter, plus extra for greasing

1 cup fine fresh white bread crumbs

1½ tbsp all-purpose flour

1¾ cups warm milk

6 oz/175 g Cheddar cheese, grated

2½ oz/70 g Gruyère cheese, grated

pinch of freshly grated nutmeg

pinch of cayenne pepper

4 pickled red or green chili peppers, drained, seeded (optional), and sliced

salt and pepper

one Preheat the oven to 400°F/200°C. Lightly grease a baking dish suitable for serving from. Bring a large pan of salted water to a boil over high heat. Stir in the macaroni and boil for 2 minutes less than the package directions. Drain, rinse under cold running water to prevent further cooking, then drain again and set aside.

two Meanwhile, melt 2 tablespoons of the butter in a medium pan over medium heat. Stir into the bread crumbs in a bowl and set aside.

three Melt the remaining butter in the same pan. Sprinkle in the flour and stir constantly for 1 minute. Remove the pan from the heat and slowly pour in the milk, whisking constantly.

four Return the pan to the heat and simmer, stirring constantly, until the sauce thickens. Remove the pan from the heat and stir in ¾ cup of the Cheddar cheese, ¼ cup of the Gruyère cheese, the nutmeg, cayenne pepper, and salt and pepper to taste, stirring until smooth.

five Add the pasta and sliced chili peppers to the sauce and stir together. Spoon the pasta into the prepared dish and spread out. Sprinkle the remaining cheeses and bread crumbs over the top. Bake in the oven for 25 minutes until golden brown on top.

did you know?

Virginian Thomas Jefferson, the third president, introduced Italian pasta to the fledgling country. He developed a taste for Italian pasta while serving as America's ambassador in Paris in the 1780s. Yet it wasn't until the 19th century that the first recipes for this uniquely American baked dish appeared in cookbooks.

Few pan-fried catfish dinners in the South are served without a portion of these golden, deep-fried cornmeal dumplings on the side. Traditionally, they are cooked in the pan that the catfish was fried in, using the same fat for extra flavor.

hush puppies

ingredients

1¾ cups yellow cornmeal
½ cup all-purpose flour, sifted
1 small onion, finely chopped
1 tbsp sugar
2 tsp baking powder

½ tsp salt
¾ cup milk
1 egg, beaten
corn oil, for deep-frying

one Stir the cornmeal, flour, onion, sugar, baking powder, and salt together in a bowl and make a well in the center.

two Beat the milk and egg together in a pitcher, then pour into the dry ingredients and stir until a thick batter forms.

three Heat at least 2 inches/5 cm of oil in a deep skillet or pan over high heat until the temperature reaches 350–375°F/180–190°C, or until a cube of bread browns in 30 seconds.

four Drop in as many teaspoonfuls of the batter as will fit without overcrowding the skillet and cook, stirring constantly, until the hush puppies puff up and turn golden.

five Remove the hush puppies from the oil with a slotted spoon and drain on paper towels. Reheat the oil, if necessary, and cook the remaining batter. Serve hot.

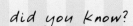

did you know?
It is said that hush puppies were given their name in the days before indoor kitchens. Busy, harassed cooks would cook cornmeal mush and toss it to begging and yelping dogs with the words, "Hush, puppy!"

Southern cooks produce notoriously rich, sweet desserts. Freshly baked pies are a regular feature of Southern menus, with Sweet Potato Pie, Key Lime Pie, and Mississippi Mud Pie among the favorites.

Peach cobbler is a down-home summer treat, while the more sophisticated flambéed Bananas Foster comes from New Orleans. To bring a Southern touch to Christmas celebrations, Bourbon Balls can be prepared a month in advance, and the coconut and orange combination in Ambrosia will provide a light and refreshing end to any indulgent meal.

desserts

prepare 30 minutes, plus 1 hour's chilling
cook about 1 hour *serves* 8–10

Serve slices of this pie and see if guests can guess the main ingredient—few people will expect the humble sweet potato to be turned into such a rich, indulgent dessert.

sweet potato pie

ingredients

1 lb 2 oz/500 g orange-fleshed
  sweet potatoes, scrubbed
3 extra-large eggs, beaten
½ cup packed brown sugar
1½ cups canned evaporated milk
3 tbsp butter, melted
2 tsp vanilla extract
1 tsp ground cinnamon
1 tsp ground nutmeg or freshly
  grated nutmeg
½ tsp salt
whipped cream, to serve

pie dough
1¼ cups all-purpose flour, plus extra
  for dusting
½ tsp salt
¼ tsp sugar
1½ tbsp butter, diced
3 tbsp white vegetable fat, diced
2–2½ tbsp ice-cold water

one To make the pie dough, sift the flour, salt, and sugar into a bowl. Add the butter and white vegetable fat to the bowl and rub in with the fingertips until fine crumbs form. Sprinkle over 2 tablespoons of the water and mix with a fork until a soft dough forms. If the dough is too dry, sprinkle in an extra ½ tablespoon of water. Wrap in plastic wrap and chill for at least 1 hour.

two Meanwhile, bring a large pan of water to a boil over high heat. Add the sweet potatoes and cook for 15 minutes. Drain, then cool them under cold running water. When cool, peel, then cut each into 8 wedges. Put the sweet potatoes into a separate bowl and beat in the eggs and sugar until very smooth. Beat in the remaining ingredients, then set aside until required.

three When ready to bake, preheat the oven to 425°F/220°C. Roll out the dough on a lightly floured counter into a thin 11-inch/28-cm circle and use to line a 9-inch/23-cm pie plate, about 1½ inches/4 cm deep. Trim off the excess dough and press the floured tines of a fork around the edge.

four Prick the base of the pastry shell all over with the fork and place crumpled kitchen foil in the center. Bake in the oven for 12 minutes until lightly golden.

five Remove the pastry shell from the oven, take out the foil, pour the filling into the shell, and return to the oven for an additional 10 minutes. Reduce the oven temperature to 325°F/160°C and bake for an additional 35 minutes, or until a knife inserted into the center comes out clean. Let cool on a wire rack. Serve warm or at room temperature with whipped cream.

The thought of a "mud pie" might not be appealing, but this chilled chocolate pie with pecans is anything but unappetizing. It is so rich that thin slices will suffice for most guests.

mississippi mud pie

ingredients

1 cup butter or margarine, plus extra
  for greasing
6 oz/175 g semisweet chocolate,
  coarsely chopped
½ cup corn syrup
4 large eggs, beaten
½ cup pecans, finely chopped
whipped cream, to serve

crumb crust
5 oz/140 g graham crackers
½ cup pecans, finely chopped
1 tbsp soft light brown sugar
½ tsp ground cinnamon
6 tbsp butter, melted

one Preheat the oven to 350°F/180°C. Lightly grease a 9-inch/23-cm springform or loose-bottom cake pan.

two To make the crumb crust, put the graham crackers, pecans, sugar, and cinnamon into a food processor and process until fine crumbs form—do not overprocess to a powder. Add the melted butter and process again until moistened.

three Tip the crumb mixture into the pan and press over the bottom and about 1½ inches/4 cm up the side of the pan. Cover the pan and let chill while making the filling.

four To make the filling, put the butter, chocolate, and corn syrup into a pan over low heat and stir until melted and blended. Let cool, then beat in the eggs and pecans.

five Pour the filling into the chilled crumb crust and smooth the surface. Bake in the oven for 30 minutes, or until just set but still soft in the center. Let cool on a wire rack. Serve at room temperature or chilled with whipped cream.

did you know?
This rich chocolate pie gets its name from the dark brown color of the filling—said to resemble the rich mud along the banks of the Mississippi.

prepare about 45 minutes, plus 2 hours' chilling
cook no cooking *serves* 4–6

For many Southern families, the Christmas Day feast isn't complete without this coconut and orange salad, served in the best cut-glass bowl. And for busy cooks, ambrosia is also ideal for entertaining at any time of the year as it can be assembled a day ahead.

ambrosia

ingredients

1 fresh coconut

3 large oranges

½ tbsp freshly squeezed lemon juice

confectioners' sugar, to taste (optional)

one To prepare the coconut, use a hammer and nail or screw to puncture the soft eyes at the top. Drain the coconut liquid into a bowl. Use the hammer to gently tap the coconut shell all round until it cracks and splits on its own. Cut the coconut meat away from the hard shell, then peel off and discard the thin brown membrane. Use a food processor or hand grater to grate 2 cups of the coconut meat, then set aside.

two Peel the oranges over a bowl to catch the juices, carefully removing all the bitter white pith. Cut the oranges into ¼-inch/5-mm slices, removing and discarding the seeds.

three Put the coconut, orange slices, reserved orange juice, and the lemon juice into a large glass serving bowl and toss together. Taste and sift over a little confectioners' sugar if the orange juice is not sweet enough, then toss again.

four Cover and let chill for at least 2 hours, tossing the ingredients together frequently and just before serving.

did you know?

Southerners were so fond of this ethereal combination that they gave it the title "ambrosia," from Greek and Roman mythology—ambrosia was the food that the gods ate to preserve their immortality. It is said that the dish originated from the time when crates of fresh oranges and/or coconuts were common Christmas gifts.

This flambéed dish, originally from Brennan's, one of the best-known restaurants in New Orleans, makes a spectacular end to any meal. The cinnamon-flavored syrup can be made in advance, ready for the flaming finale.

bananas foster

ingredients

1 cup dark brown sugar

½ cup butter, diced

1 tsp ground cinnamon

4 firm bananas, cut in half lengthwise
   and sliced

4 scoops premium-quality vanilla
   ice cream

4 tbsp rum

1 tbsp bourbon

one Put the sugar, butter, and cinnamon into a large skillet over high heat and heat, stirring constantly, until the sugar and butter melt. Cook, stirring constantly, for 3–4 minutes until a golden brown syrup forms.

two Stir the bananas into the syrup, gently turning the slices until they are coated and heated through. Meanwhile, put a scoop of ice cream into each of 4 individual heatproof serving bowls.

three Heat the rum and bourbon in a long-handled ladle then ignite. Pour the flaming spirits into the banana mixture, then immediately spoon the banana mixture over the ice cream and serve at once.

did you know?

Although bananas foster is often served as a dessert, the recipe was devised in the 1950s as part of a "Breakfast at Brennan's" brunch promotion—a tradition that continues today with table-side flambéing. Bananas foster has become so popular that it now appears on menus throughout the South, especially in Florida.

prepare 20 minutes, plus 2½ hours' cooling and chilling
cook 20 minutes *serves* 8

Tart and creamy, this classic American pie is ideal for summer entertaining. Commercial key limes pies have green food coloring added, but this recipe is undoctored and has a pale cream color.

key lime pie

ingredients

1¾ cups canned sweetened
  condensed milk
½ cup freshly squeezed lime juice
finely grated rind of 3 limes
4 large egg yolks
whipped cream, to serve

crumb crust
6 oz/175 g graham crackers or
  gingersnap cookies
2 tbsp superfine sugar
½ tsp ground cinnamon
2½ oz/70 g butter, melted

one Preheat the oven to 325°F/160°C. Lightly grease a 9-inch/23-cm pie plate, about 1½ inches/4 cm deep.

two To make the crumb crust, put the graham crackers, sugar, and cinnamon into a food processor and process until fine crumbs form—do not overprocess to a powder. Add the melted butter and process again until moistened.

three Tip the crumb mixture into the pie plate and press over the bottom and up the side. Place the pie plate on a baking sheet and bake in the oven for 5 minutes.

four Meanwhile, beat the condensed milk, lime juice, lime rind, and egg yolks together in a bowl until well blended.

five Remove the crumb crust from the oven, pour the filling into the crumb crust and spread out to the edge. Return to the oven for an additional 15 minutes, or until the filling is set around the edge but still wobbly in the center. Let cool completely on a wire rack, then cover and let chill for at least 2 hours. Serve with dollops of whipped cream.

did you know?

This pie dates from the late 1850s, after canned condensed milk became available—a welcome development in the remote Florida Keys, where fresh milk was a luxury. Key limes aren't commercially grown elsewhere and their season is short, so ordinary limes are most frequently used in this all-American favorite.

Summertime in Georgia means one thing—peaches, peaches, and more peaches. This old-fashioned baked dessert with its "cobblestone" topping is a traditional way to take advantage of the seasonal glut.

peach cobbler

ingredients

6 peaches, peeled and sliced
  (see Cook's Tip)
4 tbsp superfine sugar
½ tbsp lemon juice
1½ tsp cornstarch
½ tsp almond or vanilla extract
vanilla or butter pecan ice cream,
  to serve

cobbler topping
1¼ cups all-purpose flour
generous ½ cup superfine sugar
1½ tsp baking powder
½ tsp salt
6 tbsp butter, diced
1 egg
5–6 tbsp whole milk

one Preheat the oven to 425°F/220°C. Put the peaches into a 9-inch/23-cm square ovenproof dish that is suitable for serving from. Add the sugar, lemon juice, cornstarch, and almond extract and toss together. Bake the peaches in the oven for 20 minutes.

two Meanwhile, to make the topping, sift the flour, all but 2 tablespoons of the sugar, the baking powder, and salt into a bowl. Rub in the butter with the fingertips until fine crumbs form. Combine the egg and 5 tablespoons of the milk in a pitcher and mix into the dry ingredients with a fork until a soft, sticky dough forms. If the dough seems dry, stir in the extra tablespoon of milk.

three Reduce the oven temperature to 400°F/200°C. Remove the peaches from the oven and drop spoonfuls of the topping over the surface, without smoothing. Sprinkle with the remaining sugar, return to the oven, and bake for an additional 15 minutes, or until the topping is golden brown and firm—the topping will spread as it cooks. Serve hot or at room temperature with ice cream on the side.

cook's tip

To peel the peaches, cut a small cross in the stem end of each peach. Lower them into a pan of boiling water and let stand for 10–30 seconds, depending on ripeness. Drain and cool under cold running water to prevent further cooking. Peel using a small knife.

"Butter pecan" is one of America's favorite ice cream flavors. This recipe from Georgia illustrates why—it is ultra-rich and sweet. Serve after a light main course, or scoop into cones for a summer treat.

butter pecan ice cream

ingredients

1½ cups heavy cream
¾ cup milk
6 egg yolks
½ cup superfine sugar

½ cup clarified butter, diced
 (see Cook's Tip)
1½ cups coarsely chopped pecans

one Bring ½ cup of the cream and the milk to a boil in a pan over medium-high heat. Remove the pan from the heat and let the mixture cool completely. Pour into a bowl, cover, and let chill for 30 minutes.

two Using an electric mixer on high speed, beat the egg yolks with 4 tablespoons of the sugar until pale and thick enough to hold a ribbon on the surface when the beaters are lifted. Set aside.

three Combine the remaining cream and sugar in the rinsed-out pan and bring just to a boil. Pour about half the hot cream into the egg mixture, beating constantly, then pour all this mixture into the pan, stirring to blend both mixtures together. Heat just until small bubbles appear around the edge. Add the clarified butter and stir until it melts.

four Pour the mixture into a bowl and let cool completely, stirring occasionally. Pour in the chilled cream-and-milk mixture and stir until blended. Pour the mixture into an ice-cream maker and freeze according to the manufacturer's directions. When it is about three-quarters frozen, stir in the nuts. Alternatively, pour the mixture into a freezerproof container, cover, and freeze for 1 hour, or until partially frozen. Remove from the freezer and beat with a fork until smooth. Re-cover and return to the freezer. Repeat the freezing and beating process, then stir in the nuts, return to the freezer, and freeze for 1½–2 hours, or until firm. Serve in individual glasses.

cook's tip

For a smooth finish, it is important to use clarified butter, which has had the milk solids removed. To make ½ cup, melt ¾ cup of butter in a pan over low heat. Remove from the heat and let the milk solids sink to the bottom. Skim off the foam, then carefully pour off the bright yellow clarified butter.

Grasshopper pie is a Southern specialty, with a chocolate crumb crust and a custardlike filling flavored and colored with green crème de menthe. This is a light, delicate dessert with the same appealing flavor.

grasshopper mousse

ingredients

2 large eggs, separated, plus 1 large egg yolk

¼ tsp cream of tartar

4 tbsp superfine sugar

2½ tbsp green crème de menthe

1 tbsp white crème de cacao

⅔ cup heavy cream

grated semisweet chocolate, to decorate

one Put the egg whites into a large bowl and, using an electric mixer, beat until they turn white and frothy. Sprinkle over the cream of tartar and continue beating until stiff peaks form.

two Add half the sugar, one tablespoon at a time, and continue beating until a stiff, glossy meringue forms. Set aside.

three Put the egg yolks into a separate large bowl with the remaining sugar and beat until they double in volume and hold a ribbon on the surface when the beaters are lifted. Add the crème de menthe and the crème de cacao and continue beating until the mixture becomes thick again, although it won't be as thick as before.

four Pour the cream over the egg yolk mixture and continue beating to whip the cream mixture until soft peaks form. Spoon the meringue over the top of the mixture and, using a large metal spoon or rubber spatula, fold in until it is just blended.

five Spoon the mousse into 6 glass serving bowls, cover, and let chill for at least 2 hours. When ready to serve, grate chocolate over the tops.

did you know?

Grasshopper pie, the original inspiration for this creamy dessert, dates from the 1950s, when a creamy after-dinner cocktail called a grasshopper was fashionable. The cocktail, the pie, and this mousse all have the same main ingredient in common—bright green crème de menthe liqueur.

prepare about 15 minutes, plus 3–4 days' standing
cook no cooking *makes* 18–20

Bourbon is king in Kentucky and—perhaps not surprisingly—it finds its way into all sorts of recipes, ranging from the classic mint juleps and barbecue sauces to these no-cook, irresistible Christmas treats.

bourbon balls

ingredients

1¼ cups crumbled vanilla wafers
¾ cup pecans, very finely chopped
½ cup confectioners' sugar, plus extra
  for coating

1½ tbsp unsweetened cocoa
2 tbsp light corn syrup
4 tbsp bourbon

one Put the wafers into a food processor and process until very fine crumbs form, almost like a powder.

two Tip the crumbs into a bowl and stir in the pecans. Sift over the sugar and cocoa, then stir together. Stir the corn syrup and bourbon together in a separate small bowl and continue stirring until the syrup dissolves, then add to the dry ingredients and stir together.

three Shape the mixture into 1-inch/2.5-cm balls and roll in sugar to coat all over. Store in an airtight container for at least 3–4 days before serving, but these can be left for up to 1 month for a more pronounced bourbon flavor.

four Just before serving, roll the bourbon balls in sugar again.

did you know?

Bourbon County, Kentucky, is home to some of America's best-known bourbon producers. Distilled from corn, bourbon has been made in the area since the late 1780s and it was originally known as just "corn." Other Southern colloquial terms for corn whiskey include "dixie nectar" and "liquid joy."

index